CW0117723S

Original title:
Firelight and Flurries

Copyright © 2024 Creative Arts Management OÜ
All rights reserved.

Author: Rafael Sterling
ISBN HARDBACK: 978-9916-94-448-6
ISBN PAPERBACK: 978-9916-94-449-3

Shadows Cast by the Dancing Flames

In the hearth, the flames do sway,
Shadows flicker, a lively play.
Whispers of warmth in the night,
Moonlit dreams take gentle flight.

Candles on Snowy Evenings

Softly glowing, candles bright,
Illuminating winter's night.
Snowflakes dance with silent grace,
Each one holds a magic place.

An Ember's Allegory in a Winter's Veil

Embers glow beneath the frost,
In their warmth, nothing is lost.
Winter's chill can still ignite,
Hope that shines through darkest night.

Brilliance in the Midst of Ice

Ice reflects a diamond's gleam,
Nature's canvas, a frozen dream.
Within the stillness, voices call,
Reminding us of life's vast thrall.

Hope's Warmth Amongst the Snowy Pines

Beneath the boughs of silent trees,
A whisper stirs the frosty air.
Each flake that falls, a gentle tease,
Promising warmth, beyond despair.

Amidst the cold, the heart takes flight,
As sunlight breaks the heavy gloom.
Through winter's cloak, a spark of light,
Brings forth a bloom from frozen tombs.

The pines stand tall, steadfast and grand,
Their evergreen a sight to see.
Hope's promise dances on the land,
In every branch, a memory.

So let the snow fall soft and deep,
For even in the frost's embrace,
A warmth within begins to seep,
Renewing dreams in winter's space.

Threads of Light Weaving Through the Flurries

In swirling flurries, light does gleam,
A gentle tapestry unfolds.
Threads of gold weave through the dream,
In winter's chill, a story told.

Each snowflake spins a tale of grace,
Dancing softly, one by one.
In their twirl, the shadows chase,
While sunbeams weave, and night is done.

A canvas bright, through icy veils,
The colors burst, a vibrant show.
In quiet woods, where silence sails,
Threads of light in flurries flow.

So let the world in white delight,
As warmth begins to stir within.
Through all the cold, we'll find our light,
Weaving hope where dreams begin.

Glows Beneath the Snowy Canopy

Soft whispers of the pines,
A blanket white and pure.
Beneath the chilly night,
A warmth that feels secure.

Frosted stars above us glow,
As shadows dance and sway.
In this enchanted world,
Our worries melt away.

Ashes and Ice: A Timeless Tale

Once in flames, now frozen low,
Echoes of past's embrace.
Memories like snowflakes fall,
Time leaves a gentle trace.

Whispers of love in winter's breath,
A story told anew.
From ashes rise, in frozen heart,
The warmth that once we knew.

Radiant Hearts in a Frozen World

In a realm of ice and frost,
Two hearts beat strong and bright.
Together through the bitter chill,
We find our spark of light.

Each touch ignites the silent air,
Like fireflies born in snow.
Radiant love shines ever true,
In this wintry glow.

Warm Embrace in a Wintry Night

Snowflakes dance on moonlit streets,
The world is hushed and still.
Wrapped in blankets, side by side,
Our hearts begin to thrill.

Outside the winds may howl and wail,
But here we're safe from harm.
In your embrace, I find my peace,
A forever's gentle balm.

Winter's Veil with a Hint of Warmth

Snowflakes dance with gentle grace,
Whispers hush in the chilly space.
Warmth escapes from fires aglow,
A heart's ember beneath the snow.

Footprints crunch on a frozen trail,
Soft laughter rides the winter's gale.
Beneath the blanket, dreams ignite,
A hidden spark in the cold, so bright.

The Glow of Confidence in the Cold

A frigid breeze can't dim the shine,
With every step, our spirits align.
Wrapped in layers, yet feeling bold,
Our laughter breaks through the biting cold.

Chill may come, but we stand tall,
With joy and strength, we conquer all.
In winter's clutch, we're finding grace,
The glow of warmth in every place.

Light's Embrace on Frosted Fields

Morning light on fields of white,
Shimm'ring crystals, pure delight.
Nature's canvas, painted bright,
A world awakened by the light.

Sunbeams dance on frosty grass,
Every shadow, a moment to pass.
In this embrace, our hearts will soar,
Finding beauty at winter's door.

A Flicker of Joy in Winter's Silence

In the stillness, moments bloom,
A flicker bright against the gloom.
Silent echoes wrap the night,
Joy ignites like stars in flight.

As snow descends, the world is hushed,
In frosty air, our spirits rushed.
Each breath whispers tales untold,
In winter's heart, pure joy unfolds.

Shimmering Flames and Frozen Dreams

In the night, the fire gleams,
Whispers dance in silver streams.
Flickering shadows rise and sway,
Lost in thoughts that drift away.

Within the blaze, our hopes ignite,
In every spark, a glimpse of light.
Yet outside waits the cold embrace,
Silent night, a frozen space.

Dreams entwined in warmth and fear,
Yearning hearts draw ever near.
Though the world is draped in white,
Shimmering flames dispel the night.

Beneath the Snow, a Warmth Still Glows

Underneath the icy crust,
Lingers softly the hopeful trust.
Hidden embers, deep and bright,
Await the kiss of spring's first light.

Whispers echo through the trees,
Stirring gently in the breeze.
Beneath the snow, a pulse does beat,
Life persists, though bittersweet.

Through the chill, there's something bold,
Stories waiting to be told.
Beneath the frost, the world will find,
A warmth that lingers, intertwined.

Serenity in the Between

In the quiet pause of day,
Where the dusk and dawn hold sway.
Moments blend in soft delight,
Between the dark and fading light.

Here, the heart can breathe and sigh,
Where the whispers softly lie.
Every second holds a chance,
In between, we learn to dance.

Stillness wraps the weary mind,
In the space, pure peace we find.
Serenity, a gentle guide,
In the in-between, we confide.

Embers in the Snow

Falling flakes, a delicate lace,
Covering the earth with grace.
Yet beneath a blanket wide,
Embers flicker, warmth inside.

As the winter winds do blow,
Silent echoes of fire's glow.
In the chill, a heart beats strong,
Whispers soft like a sweet song.

Even when the world feels cold,
Carry dreams, be brave, be bold.
For within the frost's bright show,
Live the embers in the snow.

Radiance Among the Falling White

Snowflakes dance in silver light,
They tumble down, so pure and bright.
Each gentle whisper, soft and low,
Embraces earth with quiet glow.

Branches laden, a frosty crown,
Nature dons her glistening gown.
In the stillness, peace unfolds,
A timeless tale in silence told.

Chasing Shadows in Winter Light

Shadows stretch, then swiftly flee,
Dancing 'neath the oak and tree.
Winter sun, a fleeting friend,
Guiding paths where lost things mend.

Footprints linger in the frost,
Memories made, but never lost.
Chasing dreams as daylight wanes,
In the hush of twilight's chains.

Sparks Amidst the Sleet

Amidst the gloom, bright embers glow,
A flicker reigns where cold winds blow.
Each spark ignites a fleeting cheer,
Warming hearts that draw them near.

Sleet cascades with icy grace,
Yet hope ignites in this harsh place.
Through the darkness, fire fights,
Filling souls with glowing lights.

Glints of Warmth in the Arctic Whisper

Whispers travel through the chill,
Carried forth on icy thrill.
Glints of warmth, a tender sigh,
As northern lights dance in the sky.

Frigid air yet softly stirs,
Each gentle breeze, a lover's purrs.
In the vastness, dreams take flight,
Wrapped in blankets of starlight.

Embers in the Twilight

In the evening's breath, soft and light,
Embers flicker, a warming sight.
Shadows stretch, the day now wanes,
Crickets sing in sweet refrains.

The horizon bleeds in hues of gold,
Whispers of stories yet untold.
Stars awake, the night draws near,
In this moment, I hold dear.

Whispers of the Winter Glow

Silent snowflakes gently fall,
Covering earth, a serene call.
The world wrapped in a blanket white,
Whispers echo through the night.

Fires crackle in steamy rooms,
A dance of warmth against the glooms.
Hot cocoa shared, laughter flows,
In winter's clutch, our friendship grows.

Dancing Shadows in the Snow

Footprints trace a tale untold,
As shadows dance in the cold.
Moonlight bathes each flake aglow,
In the night, where dreams may flow.

Ski tracks zigzag, a playful run,
Nature's canvas, so much fun.
Laughter rises, echoes play,
In winter's realm, we glide away.

Warmth Beneath the Frost

Underneath the icy crust,
Life pulses with unyielding trust.
Roots reach deep, in dark embrace,
While winter holds a solemn space.

Yet springs will come, as surely they must,
Awakening dreams, igniting the dust.
Buds will bloom, and colors will burst,
From warmth beneath, an endless thirst.

Serenity in the Softest Light

In the dawn's gentle glow,
Whispers of dreams take flight,
Morning's embrace feels slow,
Wrapped in the softest light.

Petals dance with the breeze,
Nature's calm lullabies,
Hearts find solace with ease,
Under the blushing skies.

Golden rays gently touch,
Quietude fills the air,
Moments that mean so much,
Serenity everywhere.

The Sizzle of Warmth Against the Arctic Breeze

Fires crackle brightly,
Against the cold, sharp teeth,
The warmth dances lightly,
In winter's frosty sheath.

Footsteps crunch on the snow,
While laughter fills the air,
The hearth pulls us to glow,
In moments that we share.

Winds whisper tales of ice,
Yet hearts stay warm within,
A magic that suffices,
Where our true joys begin.

Snowflakes and Sparks in a Whirlwind

In the swirl of winter's breath,
Snowflakes dance with flair,
Caught in nature's wild wreath,
Twinkling without a care.

Sparks from the fire ignite,
Chasing shadows away,
Illuminating the night,
In a shimmering play.

Wind carries soft laughter,
Through the chilly expanse,
An embrace of what comes after,
In the joy of each chance.

A Bloomsong of Heat in a Cold Retreat

In the quiet of nightfall,
Blossoms awaken with grace,
Heat whispers a soft call,
In this frost-kissed place.

Petals warm against chill,
Their colors bold and bright,
Nature's canvas does thrill,
In the dim evening light.

A symphony of delight,
As the world stands so still,
Each bloom a spark, a sight,
Filling the heart with thrill.

Glimmers of Light on Chilly Eves

The stars above begin to gleam,
While shadows dance in moonlit beam.
A whisper of warmth fills the air,
With flickers of hope, joys to share.

As frost-kissed breaths create a trace,
Each crystal spark finds its place.
With laughter echoing through the night,
Glimmers of dreams set hearts alight.

Some cozy corners glow so bright,
Embracing love against the night.
Hot cocoa swirls in tender hands,
Each sip a tale that warmth demands.

A gentle hush wraps the town,
As snowflakes twirl softly down.
In silence, beauty takes its flight,
Glimmers of wishes under the night.

A Dance of Heat and Ice

In the cradle of winter, warmth blooms,
As firelight sways, casting rooms.
Chill meets warmth in a playful chase,
Together they dance, finding grace.

Breath of fog rolls through the glen,
Icicles gleam, kissed by zen.
The heart beats fast with every glance,
In this timeless, swirling dance.

Steam rises high, a swirling mist,
While frost finds solace, a gentle tryst.
Textures collide, a vibrant show,
Heat and ice, a wondrous flow.

Together they weave a tapestry bright,
Creating mosaics in vivid light.
A joy in the clash, a thrill in the blend,
A dance everlasting, no need to pretend.

Flicker and Flurry Until Dawn

Snowflakes drift in swirling flight,
As shadows play in soft moonlight.
A fire crackles, whispers of cheer,
While dreams unfurl, crystal clear.

Each flicker of warmth, a refuge found,
In winter's arms, hearts gather round.
Laughter and stories dance with ease,
While outside the world wears a winter's freeze.

Stars wink down as night unfolds,
Peaceful moments, warm as gold.
Together we share this magical time,
In flicker and flurry, we find our rhyme.

Until dawn breaks, we'll hold the night,
In whispers low, everything feels right.
Wrapped in the glow of our embrace,
Flicker and flurry, a timeless space.

Winter's Breath on a Welcoming Glow

Crisp air whispers secrets anew,
As winter's breath paints the world blue.
Along the path, the lanterns shine,
Inviting all to feel divine.

The candles flicker, shadows sway,
In cozy corners, dreams do play.
Stories unfold near the fire's warm light,
Soft whispers carry through the night.

Snow blankets earth with a silken sheet,
While laughter dances, a joyful beat.
Winter's embrace is tender and slow,
In every heartbeat, a welcoming glow.

As the night deepens, joy takes flight,
Each moment cherished within the night.
In harmony, we sigh and unfold,
Winter's breath, a tale still untold.

Glistening Heat in a Winter's Dream

In the silence of the night,
A warmth spreads, pure delight.
Snowflakes dance in twinkling light,
Dreams ignite, hearts take flight.

Reflections on the window pane,
Whispers soft, sweet refrain.
Echoes of a summer's gain,
In this chill, love shall remain.

Candles flicker, shadows play,
Hope ignites in shades of gray.
As winter's grip begins to sway,
Glistening heat will find its way.

Beneath the stars, a secret glow,
Winds of change begin to blow.
In this dream, we both will know,
Together, warmth will only grow.

Bonfire Dreams in a Blustery Night

The flames dance in swirling wind,
Tales of warmth and laughter pinned.
Around the fire, hearts rescind,
All worries fade, sweet dreams begin.

Crisp leaves swirl in a wild flight,
The world transforms in gentle light.
Voices blend, a pure delight,
Bonfire dreams embrace the night.

Marshmallows melt, sweet and gold,
Stories shared, both young and old.
In this glow, our hearts unfold,
Magic felt as dreams take hold.

As the chill wraps us in veils,
Unity prevails, love never fails.
In blustery nights, our tale regales,
Together we stand, in warmth it sails.

Shimmering Nights and Frostbitten Dreams

In shimmering nights under silk skies,
Frostbitten dreams begin to rise.
Whispers dance in gentle sighs,
Magic lingers where hope lies.

The moon hangs like a silver coin,
Breath of winter, crisp and fine.
Stars ignite in a cosmic join,
Amongst the frost, our hearts entwine.

Snowflakes twirl in playful flight,
Painting dreams in soft twilight.
In this chill, the world's polite,
Yet warmth awaits through the night.

Together we tread, hand in hand,
In frostbitten dreams, love expands.
Shimmering nights, where moments stand,
A world transformed, a treasure planned.

The Soft Glow of Candlelit Snows

The soft glow in candle's embrace,
Illuminates the winter space.
Outside, the snowflakes gently trace,
A serene hush, a tranquil pace.

Fires crackle with tales of old,
In the warmth, hearts never cold.
Magic whispers, love behold,
In our arms, memories unfold.

Twinkling lights in frosty nights,
Shadows dancing, warm delights.
Candlelit snows bring pure insights,
As we share our dreams and sights.

Together we chase the dreams ahead,
With candlelight, no fear or dread.
In this wonder, we both are led,
Through the soft glow, our hearts are fed.

Frosted Whispers and Warm Embraces

In the hush of winter's breath,
Whispers dance on frosty air.
Embraces wrap like woven warmth,
Hearts entwined in frosted care.

Snowflakes twirl in moonlit grace,
Softly settling on the ground.
Laughter echoes in the chill,
While cozy fires crackle sound.

The warmth inside, a gentle glow,
As winter's secrets softly fold.
Life embraces what we know,
In stories shared, both new and old.

Frosted branches, silver lace,
Kisses from the quiet night.
In this space, we find our place,
A love that warms the coldest site.

Cozy Moments in the Blustering Gale

The wind howls outside our door,
Yet here we sit, snug and tight.
Blankets wrap, a gentle score,
Softly glowing in the night.

Tea steams, a comforting brew,
Laughter spills like autumn leaves.
With every gust, our hearts renew,
In shared moments, joy believes.

Outside, the world may twist and turn,
But here, the flame of love stays bright.
In cozy corners, hearts will burn,
Against the bluster, we take flight.

Every sigh, a whispered dream,
Each glance, a promise woven tight.
Together in this wild esteem,
Creating warmth from winter's plight.

The Flicker of Soft Memories

Flickering flames, a gentle glow,
Memories dance like shadows cast.
Whispers of laughter come and go,
In the warmth, we've found our past.

Time captured in a fleeting glance,
The echo of a soft embrace.
In quiet moments, we take chance,
To weave our love in time and space.

Every smile, a cherished spark,
Illuminating dusky lanes.
Where once was light, now lingers dark,
Yet still, our heart's warmth remains.

In the corners of our mind,
The flicker shows us where we've been.
Soft memories, so sweetly kind,
Remind us love's the greatest win.

Glow and Chill: A Harmonious Dance

In twilight's grace, the glow unfolds,
As the chill of night descends.
Stars shimmer like whispered gold,
While the earth in silence blends.

A dance of shadows, warm and cold,
Each moment crafted, hand in hand.
In harmony, we brave the bold,
Underneath the vast night's span.

Embrace the warmth, but feel the chill,
As seasons shift and time will sway.
In nature's rhythm, lasting thrill,
We find our place, come what may.

So let the glow of love enhance,
The crisp embrace of autumn's breath.
Together weaving life's great dance,
In every heartbeat, love's soft chest.

The Glow of Solace and Silence

In the stillness of the night,
Whispers softly take their flight.
Moonlight dances on the ground,
Where peace and solace can be found.

Stars above, a gentle guide,
In their light, I will confide.
Breaths of calm and thoughts that rest,
Wrapped in night, I feel so blessed.

Echoes fade, the world's at bay,
In this quiet, I find my way.
Serene moments hold me tight,
In the glow of silent night.

Flames of Comfort in a Winter Wonderland

Snowflakes fall, a soft embrace,
Fires crackle, a warm space.
Hot cocoa swirls in mugs we hold,
As winter tales of warmth unfold.

Frosty windows, a glimpse inside,
With loved ones gathered, hearts collide.
The evening's glow, a bright delight,
In this wonderland, we ignite.

With every laugh, the flames do dance,
In cozy corners, we take a chance.
Through winter's chill, we find our way,
In flames of comfort, we choose to stay.

Chasing Shadows through the Snow

Footprints lead where shadows play,
Through drifts of white, we roam today.
Laughter echoes, spirits high,
Chasing shadows as they fly.

A winter's hush, a dreamy scene,
Merging forms where we have been.
Fleeting glimpses, time slips past,
In this wonder, moments last.

With every step, the cold winds blow,
Yet warmth blooms in the heart's soft glow.
Side by side, through winter we go,
Chasing shadows, drifting slow.

Sparks that Ignite the Quiet Night

In the hush, a spark ignites,
Flickering flames, a dance of lights.
Whispers weave through darkened skies,
As dreams awaken, softly arise.

Stars twinkle like distant fire,
In the night, we dare aspire.
With every breath, we share our plight,
In the warmth, we feel the light.

Through the quiet, we find our way,
Sparks of hope guide night to day.
In this moment, hearts take flight,
Together, we ignite the night.

Tapestry of Warmth and Cold Whispers

In the hush of winter's breath,
Warmth weaves through the cold,
Threads of laughter, light and mirth,
In the stories we unfold.

Beneath the frost, whispers cry,
Secrets held in frozen air,
Echoes of a tender sigh,
Hopes entwined in silver glare.

Gentle flames dance in the dark,
Illuminating heart's embrace,
Such moments leave a radiant mark,
In the chill, we find our place.

Embers glow against the night,
Bridging warmth with winter's chill,
In our hearts, we hold the light,
As whispers of the past fulfill.

Auroras of Warmth on a Snowy Canvas

Dazzling hues in midnight skies,
Ignite the frosty veil of white,
Nature's brush, a sweet surprise,
Painting dreams with gentle light.

Crisp air holds the magic sweet,
As stars shimmer, softly sigh,
Curved paths where warm hearts meet,
Underneath the vast, wide sky.

Snowflakes fall like whispers fair,
Cradling the warmth within,
The dance of spirits on the air,
Where love and wonder begin.

In this sight, our souls do bask,
Wrapped in beauty, pure embrace,
With every beam, we need not ask,
For warmth shall find its rightful place.

The Flicker of Hope in White-Washed Calm

In the quiet, soft and mild,
Hope flickers like a candle's glow,
A beacon kind, a tender child,
Guiding us through winter's woe.

Blankets of snow cradle the night,
Silencing thoughts of the past,
While dreams take wing in gentle flight,
In the calm, our hearts hold fast.

Each lessening storm, a promise new,
Chasing shadows, bright as day,
Through chilled air, the warmest hue,
Shimmers in this frosty ballet.

Hold this moment, breathe it in,
As the flicker dances bright,
In white-washed calm, we begin,
To find our way, to find our light.

Glowing Reflections on Icy Waters

Rippling waters, calm and clear,
Reflecting warmth beneath the ice,
In this stillness, hearts draw near,
As twilight casts its soft entice.

The glimmers dance like distant stars,
Painting tales of hope and grace,
While echoes of the past leave scars,
In the shadows, we find our space.

Moonlight kisses frigid waves,
A moment shared, a quiet thought,
Through shimmering paths, the heart craves,
Each memory held, each lesson taught.

Glowing hues on icy streams,
Secrets held in nature's sway,
In the stillness, we weave dreams,
As reflections guide our way.

Kindling Hearts in Frost's Grasp

In the quiet of the night,
Whispers dance in silver light.
Glimmers twinkle, stars ignite,
Hearts awaken, taking flight.

Frosted branches softly sigh,
Nature's breath, a gentle cry.
Warmth ignites beneath the sky,
Kindling dreams that seldom die.

The chill embraces, yet inside,
Burning flames of hope abide.
Through the cold, we find our stride,
Hand in hand, we will not hide.

With every thaw, our spirits bloom,
Love's sweet fragrance, banishing gloom.
Together, we will chase the room,
Where warmth and kindness find their home.

The Ember's Tale in Glacial Realms

In the heart of icy lands,
Fires smolder, drawn by hands.
Embers flicker, dreams expand,
Tales of warmth in snowy strands.

Glacial winds may chill the bones,
Yet the fire speaks in tones.
Stories whispered, soft as moans,
Uniting hearts as one, not lone.

Through the frost, a fire glows,
Carving pathways, melting woes.
In this realm where nobody knows,
The ember's tale of love flows.

As the stars begin to gleam,
Fires burn with a quiet dream.
In the night, they intertwine,
A tapestry of souls, divine.

Nights of Both Glimmer and Chill

Underneath a blanket bright,
Stars are twinkling, pure delight.
In the shadows, cold takes flight,
Yet love's warmth ignites the night.

Moonlight dances on the snow,
Painting dreams in silver glow.
Every heartbeat starts to flow,
In the chill, our spirits grow.

Whispers ride the evening breeze,
Telling tales of hearts at ease.
Nights of joy, they bring such peace,
In frosty air, our worries cease.

With every breath, a spark we find,
Glimmers woven in the mind.
Together, warmth and frost entwined,
In this world, our hearts confined.

Capturing the Glow in a Glistening World

In a world where shadows play,
Glistening dreams come out to sway.
Moments captured, bright and gay,
Fires flicker, lighting the way.

Snowflakes dance like drops of light,
Every sparkle feels so right.
In this glow, fears take flight,
Shining paths through endless night.

Together we embrace the scene,
Radiant hearts, healthy and keen.
In the stillness, we convene,
A world aglow, pure and serene.

With each touch, we harvest grace,
In laughter, find our rightful place.
Capturing warmth in life's embrace,
Together, we will share this space.

Comfort Cradled in Snowy Arms

In drifting flakes, the world grows still,
A gentle hush, a soft-spun thrill.
The earth adorned in winter's lace,
Embraced by cold, a warm embrace.

Silent whispers wrap the night,
Comfort found in soft twilight.
The stars peek through, a distant glow,
Cradled close, we let time slow.

In this tranquility we stay,
Cozy hearts in gentle fray.
Snowflakes dance, a twirling song,
Where peaceful souls forever long.

Together here, as dreams ignite,
We fold into the quiet night.
With snowy arms, the world will sway,
In comfort found, we'll drift away.

Light and Chill: The Duality of the Night

In whispers low, the night unfolds,
A tale of warmth and chill retold.
The moonlight bathes the world in grace,
While shadows play in hidden space.

Stars shimmer bright, a dazzling sight,
Yet frosty breath reveals the bite.
Within the dark, a spark ignites,
The dance of dreams and cozy nights.

Light and chill in twirling waltz,
A fusion found in stark contrasts.
We find our way through darkened streets,
Where laughter and the heartbeat meets.

In this balance, life's truth we trace,
The warm and chill, an endless chase.
Under stars, we'll always roam,
Finding light, we shape our home.

The Heat of Home in a Frozen Landscape

Outside the world holds winter's breath,
Fields carpeted in crystal death.
But inside walls, a blaze ignites,
Warmth spills forth on frigid nights.

The flicker of flames, a golden hue,
Wraps around hearts, tender and true.
Cocoa steams from porcelain cups,
In gentle sips, the spirit pulls up.

With laughter's echo filling the air,
Each moment savored, without a care.
In a frozen realm, together we shine,
The heat of home, a love divine.

Each snowy branch tells tales anew,
Yet in our haven, dreams come true.
Through winter's chill, we stand strong,
With warmth and love, we all belong.

The Warm Invitation of the Winter's Night

The doors ajar, a beckoning light,
Invites the weary into the night.
Frosted windows, a canvas bright,
A world transformed, a stunning sight.

Chill in the air, yet warmth within,
Where memories linger and stories begin.
Laughter echoes through cozy halls,
As winter's magic gently calls.

Under blankets, all snug and tight,
Shared moments glisten, hearts take flight.
The winter winds may howl and sigh,
But here together, we'll laugh and cry.

The stars above wink in delight,
While we gather close, holding tight.
With winter's charm, we find our way,
In warm invitations, we choose to stay.

Glistening Stars Above the Warmth Below

Above the world, stars twinkle bright,
Whispers of dreams in velvet night.
Together they dance, a celestial show,
Painting the sky with a shimmering glow.

Beneath their watch, a hearth does gleam,
Crackling flames in a soft, warm beam.
Hearts gather close, in laughter and cheer,
Shielded from cold, with loved ones near.

The stars draw near, in a cosmic embrace,
Every twinkle a wish in this sacred space.
As warmth surrounds, the night feels right,
In the glow of the stars, hearts take flight.

So let the heavens whisper and sigh,
While the warmth below holds us high.
Together we thrive in this world so wide,
With glistening stars as our guide.

A Hearth of Hope in Frigid Air

Amidst the frost and chilling breeze,
Stands a hearth, where worries freeze.
The flames dance bright, casting their glow,
Warming spirits in the night's cool flow.

With every crackle, hope ignites,
A beacon of joy on longer nights.
Gathered around, we share our tales,
In the warmth of love, the heart prevails.

Outside the world may tremble in fright,
But here we bask in glowing light.
Shadows retreat, we laugh and play,
In this circle of warmth, we find our way.

So let the cold winds wander and roam,
For we've built a place we can call home.
With every laugh, and every prayer,
We find our strength in frigid air.

The Glow of Nightfall on Snow-Covered Earth

Snowflakes fall like whispers of peace,
Blanketing the earth, a soft fleece.
Under the sky, dusk takes its hold,
Crafting a world of silver and gold.

The glow of night wraps all around,
As stars emerge, their love profound.
Each flake reflects the moon's embrace,
A shimmering dance in this tranquil space.

Footsteps silent on the powdery way,
Lost in thoughts at the end of day.
In the hush of night, dreams take flight,
Awakening wonders in soft twilight.

So let us stroll, hand in hand,
Across this snowy, enchanted land.
For in the glow, our hearts gleam bright,
In the embrace of cold, we find our light.

Spheres of Light in a Sea of White

In the stillness, lights begin to spark,
Floating softly, creating a mark.
Spheres of light in a sea of white,
Guide us gently through the night.

Each orb a beacon, shining so clear,
Radiating warmth, casting out fear.
Among the drift of winter's delight,
We chase the shadows, welcoming light.

Waves of softness, a winter's embrace,
With every glow, we find our place.
Together we wander, side by side,
In this wonder, our hearts abide.

So we'll dance under the moon's soft gaze,
Wrapped in the beauty of winter's phase.
For in this realm, so pure and bright,
We become one with spheres of light.

Whirling Flames and Soft Snow

Whirling flames dance in the night,
Casting shadows, a flickering light.
Soft snowflakes drift from above,
Filling the world with quiet love.

The warmth of fire, a gentle embrace,
While snow coats the trees with delicate lace.
Together they twirl in a winter's dream,
An enchanting scene, a perfect theme.

Sparks fly high, a radiant show,
Against the stillness of the soft snow.
In this moment, time stands still,
A harmony forged by nature's will.

In the crackle, there's a story told,
Of warmth in winter's grasp, brave and bold.
Whirling flames and soft snow combine,
Creating a beauty, simply divine.

The Light that Warms the Shivering Quiet

In the hush of dusk, a glow breaks free,
A beacon of warmth, a sight to see.
It chases the shadows of the cold night,
Bringing forth comfort, a tender light.

The shivering quiet, now gently warmed,
By the glow of love, brightly adorned.
Each flicker whispers of stories old,
In the heart of winter, a warmth to hold.

Through the stillness, hearts draw near,
As hope ignites, banishing fear.
That light, a promise, ever near,
In the darkest times, it is clear.

For in the moments when silence reigns,
The light that warms, sweetly remains.
A reminder that even in the chill,
Fires of love can embolden the will.

Glowing Trails Beneath the Blizzard

Under the blizzard, a soft glow spreads,
Lighting the path where the brave man treads.
Each step a journey through the white haze,
With glowing trails that shine and amaze.

Drifts of snow swirl like whispers in flight,
As he trudges onward, a brave sight.
The blizzard roars, wild and bold,
Yet the glowing trails tell stories untold.

In the face of storms, a warm, guiding hue,
Leading the lost, steady and true.
Under the howling, beneath all the fray,
The glowing trails light the way.

Through frosted air and swirling snow,
Hope flickers softly, a radiant glow.
In the chaos, a calm can be found,
With glowing trails, love knows no bound.

Gentle Radiance on Icy Moors

On icy moors, under the pale moon,
Gentle radiance sings a soft tune.
Silver beams dance on the frozen land,
A delicate touch by nature's hand.

The world is hushed, wrapped in still grace,
As the light caresses each tranquil space.
Whispers of winter glide through the night,
In the gentle radiance, pure and bright.

Among the frost, spirits awaken,
In the glow of the night, they're not forsaken.
Each shimmering moment, a magical sight,
Bringing warmth to the heart, a serene light.

Through the chill, warmth softly flows,
In the icy moors, gentle radiance glows.
A promise of peace in the night's embrace,
Where stillness and beauty find their place.

Hearthside Serenade

Crackling flames dance in the night,
Warmth enfolds the heart so tight.
Stories woven in soft glow,
Whispers of love wrapped in the flow.

Outside, the chill bites at the air,
Yet here, we find our sweet repair.
With every tune that softly plays,
Lost in the magic of these days.

Embers fade but echoes remain,
In every laughter, joy, and pain.
Together we share this sacred space,
Hearthside dreams we gently trace.

So let the world outside be cold,
Within these walls, our hearts unfold.
In harmony, our spirits rise,
Hearthside serenade beneath the skies.

Melodies in the Snowfall

Snowflakes twirl like dancers free,
Each a note in winter's spree.
Silence wrapped in a soft white coat,
Nature's choir begins to float.

Gentle whispers touch the ground,
In this stillness, peace is found.
Harmony in flake and frost,
In the beauty, we are lost.

Footsteps crunching, soft and slow,
Carving paths in purest glow.
Melodies of winter play,
In the twilight's fading day.

Underneath the silver light,
Dreams take flight in the quiet night.
With every breath, the cold we share,
Melodies linger, sweet and rare.

Ashes and Shivers

Flickering embers in the air,
Whispers of warmth, a distant prayer.
Ashes fall like memories stray,
Each a reflection of yesterday.

Winter's chill bites through the seam,
Shivers run deep, unravel the dream.
Yet within the heart, a fire glows,
Through the darkness, a soft light shows.

Haunted by echoes of the past,
In shadows long, we find our cast.
With every shiver, a story unfolds,
In ashes, the warmth of the bold.

So gather close, let spirits sing,
Of love that's lost and the hope it brings.
Out of the cold, our souls entwine,
In ashes and shivers, we find the divine.

Luminous Echoes of the Cold

Stars above in the midnight sky,
Shimmer like whispers, drifting high.
Luminous trails in the frozen air,
Remind us to pause, to dream, to care.

Chill wraps around, a silken embrace,
In the stillness, we find our place.
Echoes linger, soft and bright,
Guiding us gently through the night.

Each breath we take, a cloud like lace,
Fleeting moments, time's sweet grace.
In the cold, our spirits unite,
Luminous echoes make the night.

Together we weave a tapestry bold,
In the warmth, we refuse to fold.
With every glance, our hearts unfold,
In luminous echoes against the cold.

Kindle of Warmth in Frosty Hues

In the heart of winter's chill,
A glow ignites, both soft and still.
The embers dance, a gentle spark,
A beacon bright within the dark.

Wrapped in layers, warmth prevails,
As frosty breath like crystal trails.
We gather close, a cherished band,
United by this glowing strand.

The snowflakes fall like whispered dreams,
While laughter flows in cozy streams.
With every sip of spiced delight,
We find our joy in frosty night.

So let the world outside be cold,
In here, we cherish tales retold.
A kindle of warmth, we hold it tight,
In this sweet haven of winter's light.

Soft Breaths of Fire Beneath the Snow

Beneath the white, a warmth resides,
In glowing hearts where love abides.
The crackling wood, a soothing sound,
In every flicker, peace is found.

The snowflakes drift, a quiet song,
While fireside shadows dance along.
We share our dreams, our hopes, our fears,
With soft breaths of fire, allays our tears.

As chill winds howl, we find our place,
In friendly faces, warmth embrace.
The hearth aglow, a magic sphere,
Where every fleeting moment's dear.

So let the frosty winds conspire,
To bring us closer to the fire.
With stories woven through the night,
Soft breaths of fire keep us bright.

Flickering Dreams in a Chilly Night

In a night wrapped in frosty lace,
The stars above find a quiet space.
Flickering dreams take flight and soar,
As winter whispers tales of yore.

The moonlight drapes a silver sheen,
On snow-clad fields, a tranquil scene.
With every breath, a cloud appears,
A soft reminder of distant years.

We seek a spark in the dark expanse,
With twinkling eyes, we take a chance.
Through chilly winds, our spirits rise,
In flickering dreams, we touch the skies.

So let the night unfold its grace,
In every heart, there's warmth to trace.
Together we'll embrace the chill,
Flickering dreams, a magic thrill.

Echoes of Comfort in Winter's Grasp

Within the grasp of winter's breath,
A stillness falls, a hint of death.
Yet in the cold, a beauty's found,
In echoes soft, our hearts resound.

The twilight glows with tender light,
As shadows weave into the night.
With every story softly shared,
The warmth within is boldly dared.

We tread on paths where silence reigns,
Through frost-kissed air, our hope remains.
In every laugh, in every sigh,
Echoes of comfort, time flies by.

So as the snow blankets the earth,
We find in cold, a hidden worth.
Hand in hand, our spirits clasp,
In echoes of comfort, winter's grasp.

Whispers of the Winter Blaze

In the hush of night so deep,
Fires crackle, secrets keep.
Snowflakes twirl in silver flight,
Whispers dance with soft moonlight.

Embers glow with a gentle grace,
Casting warmth in this still space.
Nature's breath, a frosty sigh,
Beneath the stars, the shadows lie.

Trees adorned with coats of white,
Shimmer softly in the light.
The world, a canvas vast and grand,
In winter's hold, we take our stand.

Echoes linger, stories told,
Of hearts that brave the bitter cold.
With each spark, a promise breaks,
In winter's hold, the spirit wakes.

Flickering Shadows on Frosted Glass

Through the window, shadows play,
Frosted glass, a cold display.
Each flickering light, a gentle tease,
Hints of warmth on winter's freeze.

The world outside, a muted tone,
Silent whispers, all alone.
Yet in the glow, a hearth's embrace,
Flickers dance with soft grace.

Children's laughter, distant cheer,
Melodies that draw us near.
In the chill, a bond confined,
Through frosted glass, hearts intertwined.

As evening falls, the darkness swells,
But warmth persists where silence dwells.
Flickering flames, a timeless art,
Illuminate the winter's heart.

The Dance of Flames and Snowflakes

Amidst the storm, the flames arise,
Snowflakes whirl beneath the skies.
A lively dance, both fierce and bright,
In winter's heart, they find their light.

Fire's glow and snow's soft kiss,
Together weave a cozy bliss.
Nature's rhythm, wild and free,
In harmony, they seem to be.

The crackling wood, the swirling air,
A fleeting moment, pure and rare.
As snowflakes twirl, the flame holds tight,
Together, they defy the night.

With every spark, a story spun,
An endless waltz, two forces one.
Through winter's grasp, they find their way,
In the dance where night meets day.

Warmth Amidst the Winter Chill

Outside the world is dressed in white,
Frosty air brings a shiver's bite.
Yet in our hearts, a fire burns bright,
Creating warmth, a pure delight.

Together wrapped in scarves so dear,
Laughter echoes, melting fear.
One cup held high, we toast to time,
Finding joy in every rhyme.

With every breath, the winter fades,
Replaced by love in soft cascades.
A symphony of hearts that blend,
Warmth that lingers, never ends.

So let the chill embrace us still,
For in our hearts, we find the thrill.
Amidst the cold, we'll stand as one,
Creating warmth until it's done.

Flickering Dreams Amidst the Chill

Whispers of warmth in frosty air,
Chasing shadows, dreams we dare.
Stars above blink softly bright,
Guiding our hopes through endless night.

Against the cold, our hearts ignite,
Flickering flames in the quiet night.
Each pause we take, each breath we mold,
Becomes a story softly told.

As winter's breath lays down its shroud,
Resilience blooms thick and proud.
In our dreams, we find a spark,
Lighting paths through the dark.

Embers dance, the night draws near,
In the chill, we conquer fear.
Together we rise, never alone,
In flickering dreams, our hearts have grown.

Glowing Hearts under a Frozen Sky

Beneath a sky of twinkling white,
Hearts aglow with pure delight.
Frozen winds may bite and tear,
But warmth prevails, a love laid bare.

Each snowy flake that softly falls,
Whispers secrets, nature calls.
Underneath the crystalline dome,
We find a quiet place called home.

In laughter shared, our spirits bloom,
Inside our hearts, dispelling gloom.
Against the chill, we brightly shine,
Two glowing souls, forever entwined.

Let the frost weave its silent song,
With love, we'll rise, we will be strong.
Underneath this frozen sky,
Together we dance, we will not cry.

Sparks Beneath the Icy Veil

Underneath a blanket, cold and tight,
Sparks are hidden, ready to ignite.
An icy veil may shroud the flame,
But deep within, we call your name.

In winter's grasp, we find a way,
With every heartbeat, night and day.
Moments shared beneath the freeze,
Are threads that bind, anchor and please.

Fires flicker, shadows play,
A dance of warmth to light the way.
Challenge the chill, embrace the fight,
Sparks beneath the veil shine bright.

Through darkened paths, we forge ahead,
Carving dreams where few have tread.
Together, always, we'll prevail,
With love our guide, beneath the veil.

Radiant Flickers in Silent Nights

In the stillness of the night,
Radiant flickers bring delight.
Stars like lanterns blink and sigh,
Guiding dreams that drift on high.

Quiet moments, whispers soft,
In the dark, our spirits loft.
Each flicker tells a tale anew,
Of warmth and hope, of me and you.

As the world sleeps under the frost,
Our glowing love will never be lost.
Through silent nights, passions ignite,
Radiant souls, in purest light.

Embrace the dawn, let dreams resound,
In every heartbeat, love is found.
Together forever, steadfast in flight,
Radiant flickers in silent night.

Lanterns in the Snowstorm

Lanterns gleam in the dark,
Their warm glow cuts the chill.
Soft whispers of the night,
Filling hearts with a thrill.

Footsteps crunch on the ground,
Each step a story unfolds.
Shimmering flakes softly fall,
Secrets that winter holds.

A dance of shadows and light,
Guided by flickering flames.
Hope shines through the storm,
Calling us by our names.

Together, we walk on and on,
As lanterns lead the way.
In the midst of the snowstorm,
We find warmth and stay.

Warmth Interwoven with Winter's Embrace

Fires crackle with delight,
In the stillness of the night.
Wrapped in blankets of care,
Moments that feel so right.

The chill bites at our cheeks,
Yet love dances in the air.
Together we sip our tea,
Finding peace beyond compare.

Stars blink through frosty panes,
Reminding us of dreams.
In winter's deep embrace,
Life is not what it seems.

Wrap me in your laughter,
As snowflakes grace the ground.
In this woven warmth of us,
True solace can be found.

The Color of Embers against a Pale Canvas

Embers glow in the night,
Painting warmth on the white.
A flicker tells a tale,
Of love's unwavering light.

The moon drapes its silver,
Above the forest so bare.
While shadows stretch and blend,
Embers whisper a prayer.

Crimson, orange, and gold,
Bud against the tundra's breath.
Together they ignite,
Defying winter's death.

Nature's canvas unfolds,
In hues both bold and bright.
Embers dance through the cold,
Filling the heart with light.

Shadows in the Snowy Hearth

Shadows flicker and sway,
In the cozy, warm glow.
The dance of memories,
In the cold, drifting slow.

Each shadow tells a tale,
Of laughter, love, and grace.
In a world wrapped in white,
Home finds its cherished place.

Whispers glide through the air,
A song of warmth and cheer.
Snow falls outside the door,
But within, all is dear.

As the hearth gently burns,
We gather, hearts entwined.
In shadows fluttering near,
Our spirit's warmth combined.

Dancing Flames Beneath a Frosted Sky

In the hearth, the flames do sway,
Glowing bright against the gray.
Whispers of warmth in the cold night,
Dancing flames, a flickering light.

Outside, the frost begins to creep,
Painting all in silence deep.
Stars above a shimmering show,
While below, the embers glow.

Each spark a story told in glow,
Of days gone by and hearts in tow.
Beneath the sky, so vast, so wide,
The heat within, our souls abide.

So let us gather, close and near,
With warm embraces, hearts sincere.
For in this dance, we find our light,
Beneath the frost, our spirits bright.

Glowing Moments in a White Wonderland

In a winter's dream, all aglow,
Soft flakes tumble down like snow.
Each whispering flurry gently falls,
In wonderland, where beauty calls.

Moments captured, crystals gleam,
Reflecting a world that feels like a dream.
The air is crisp, each breath a song,
In this frost, we know we belong.

Children's laughter, pure delight,
Creating memories, hearts so light.
With every step on the powdery white,
We weave our joy, sparkling bright.

Under moonlight, shadows dance,
In this magic, we take a chance.
Together, as the stars align,
We feel the warmth, our hearts entwine.

Hearthstone Memories Under Frost

By the hearth's soft, glowing face,
Memories linger in warm embrace.
Crackling wood and stories share,
Rays of warmth in winter's glare.

Snowflakes settle on windowpanes,
Nature's beauty in frosty chains.
Each moment cherished, every smile,
Time stands still, if just a while.

The laughter shared, a radiant glow,
As outside, the chilly winds do blow.
With every flicker, we reminisce,
In the warmth of love, pure bliss.

So let the storms howl, let them call,
Inside, we gather, standing tall.
Hearthstone memories hold us tight,
Kindled warmth through the frosty night.

The Chill of Night and the Warmth Within

In the hush of night, the chill descends,
But within our hearts, the warmth transcends.
Wrapped in blankets, stories unfold,
In whispered tones, our memories told.

The moonlight dances on frosty glass,
While time drifts slowly, moments pass.
Each breath a cloud in the cool air,
Yet here in the glow, we do not care.

With laughter echoing through the dark,
We find our way, igniting a spark.
For every chill that the night bestows,
The warmth within, love always grows.

Together we face the frosty night,
Hand in hand, hearts shining bright.
For in this dance, both sweet and true,
The chill of night brings warmth anew.